LOL *

*Little Old Ladies
Laughing Out Loud

An irreverent look at love, life and growing older

by Lesley Reifert

Dedication

This is for all my girlfriends who shared their stories, who laughed and cried over life's twists and turns, and who made it possible for me to write about them.

Many thanks to my friend, Sandy Rosen, who helped with the editing, Rachel Torda for her graphics expertise, and to my husband Richard who always inspires me.

CONTENTS

The Body Beautiful

The Facts of Wife

The Change of Life

Technologically Challenged

Memory Lane

Musings

THE
BODY
BEAUTIFUL

The Wonder of it All

I used to be a willowy five-six in stocking feet.

Now I'm barely five foot four, and only if I cheat.

I also weighed a good bit less than I do today.

I've gained so much that just last week I threw my scale away.

I shop the "women's sizes" now, instead of "junior miss."

I look at family photographs and tend to reminisce

about the days when I was thin and had a slender waist.

Nowadays, elastic pants are much more to my taste.

My mother always told me that it wasn't nice to fib,

but when I'm lying to myself, I've gotten very glib.

I tell myself that I'm not big. They changed the sizing charts.

And I need larger blouses since they're now made without darts.

But I can brag about my bra; it's smaller than before.

In dollars, though, I've found it's true that less is really more.

I'm paying more for lacy cup and size enhancing lift

to fight the laws of gravity, if you get my drift.

My waist has sagged, my hips have drooped,

my cellulite has dropped.

But thanks to Wonder Bra® my breasts

are permanently propped.

Thong Song

Bras are hard to buy these days. Just when I find the perfect fit,

I go to buy another and they've discontinued it.

The same thing goes for underpants. I loved a cotton brief.

Now, they're high cut, nylon wisps, or thongs that give me grief.

I'm glad we gave up girdles, and long line bras and such,

but prancing 'round in g strings at my age is way too much.

I like a sexy camisole, and lacy satin slips,

but couldn't they use cotton for the cloth that girds my hips?

These days, I'm all for comfort, for usefulness and fit.

But maybe I should buy a thong, just for the fun of it.

It looks good on the mannequin that's up there on display,

but who would see me showing off my sexy lingerie?

I sigh, select some briefs and head off to the checkout desk.

Those thongs weren't really made for anyone who's Rubenesque.

Gravitas

The laws of gravity,
I can see
apply to more
than an apple tree.

Standing in front of
a full length mirror,
I have a feeling
akin to terror.

'Round my middle, as
plain as can be,
gravity has
surrounded me.

Mail Order Blues

My junk mail is increasing a little more each day,

especially the catalogs in larger print display,

of things to help us seniors like a cane, a vitamin

designed for over-sixty folks, much to my chagrin.

Why do they mail these things to me?

They're things that I don't need.

In fact, the catalogs are mail that I don't really read.

I just look at the pictures. They give me such a thrill.

They prove that though I'm aging, I'm not yet o'er the hill.

I may have some arthritis, some varicosities,

sagging boobs and crows feet, bursitis in my knees.

I may be just a bit past prime to be a centerfold,

but I don't need a catalog to prove I'm getting old.

Long Nose Longing

Except for lines and wrinkles, as far as my face goes,

I wouldn't change a thing except I need a longer nose.

To read fine print, I have to push my glasses down a bit,

and down is not quite far enough to read, I must admit.

I wish I were Pinocchio. I'd change its length at will.

But fixing body parts like that would take a lot of skill.

Yet if I learned to do that, by accident sublime,

the men in town would find my door and get here double time.

They'd be begging me for help to make them grow a bit.

And I'd agree to help them for their sweethearts' benefit.

The Mayor would bestow me with the key to our fair city,

voted and decided on by all in the committee.

I'd be a hero to the town, in my fantasy,

and all this came about because of what I couldn't see.

I guess I'll get new glasses. That's easier, I suppose,

but if I could, I really would prefer a longer nose.

The Real Thing

My knees are stiff, my hair is thin,

I've age spots on each hand.

I wear my years with scars to show

life doesn't go as planned.

I've lost a friend, and lost a job,

and gained a pound or two,

but I keep going, anyway.

That's all that I can do.

Now my philosophy remains:

in this life, love a lot,

and even if you're up in age,

you'll still look young and hot.

But while you're thinking sexy thoughts

(an aphrodisiac?)

remember what the *real* thing does

to your sacroiliac.

Padded Bras

Time was when I was young and bolder,
I couldn't wait to look lots older.
I'd stick some tissues in my bra,
wear dark mascara, and, voila,
I'd practice gazing o'er my shoulder
my very best "come hither" smolder.
I'd simper down the hall at school,
thinking I looked oh, so cool,
and pray for boys to notice me.
I swam in sexuality.
In fashion, I broke every rule.
I wanted all the boys to drool.
Now in my waning years I still
put tissues in my bra to fill
the empty space and keep them near,
to wipe my nose or dry a tear.
Enlarging boobs when I'm over the hill
would be somewhat like overkill.
My eyes are dark from lack of sleep;
it does no good to count some sheep.

If I could go back to my youth,

I'd partake of less vermouth,

I'd wear less make-up. Never weep.

Watch my weight, and get more sleep.

I'd diet more and exercise,

and never, ever supersize

my fries or burgers on the run.

I wouldn't even eat the bun.

Looking back, it sounds so wise,

but that's because I fantasize.

In truth, I'd do it all again,

especially when it comes to men.

All it took to catch a guy

were larger breasts and a tender sigh.

It seemed so simple, way back then,

buying make-up at the five and ten.

If I could do things differently

to get the guys to notice me,

if I could change, just like the Phoenix,

I'd definitely buy more Kleenex®.

The Golden Years

Time was, I'd spring up from the bed.

Now, I tend to wait instead,

to see if all my joints are working,

or feel if any pain is lurking.

And if it's going to rain, my bones

will let me know with creaks and groans.

Once I'm sure each body part

is functioning, my day can start.

I swing my legs down to the floor,

and head right through the bathroom door.

Yet in the mirror, watching me

is not the chick I used to be,

with long brown curls and flashing eyes,

but some old woman in disguise.

Every day there's another wrinkle,

even before my morning tinkle.

Whoever called these "golden years"

had more than wax inside their ears.

"Gold" to me means wealth untold.

"Golden years" means growing old.

Survival Skills

The lines of experience
show on my face.
The etchings reflect how
I'm aging with grace.
They tell how I've laughed,
how I've wept in my grief,
how I've loved and been loved,
all in stark bas relief.
I could get a facelift,
the wrinkles to hide,
but that wouldn't fix
all the feelings inside.
I've earned all these wrinkles,
and each one is dear.
They say I've survived for
at least one more year.

Aids Generation

I've a thing in my ear to help me hear,

a cane to help me walk,

a set of false teeth I wear so you

understand me when I talk.

My glasses sit on my nose all day

so I can see to read.

I can't believe the aids I use

I didn't used to need.

My senses all need so much help.

I have this revelation.

Aside from sex, this really is

a new "aids" generation.

Plastic Surgery

If I won the lottery,

with any luck,

I'd have plastic surgery,

a tummy tuck,

I'd lift up my eyelids,

and get my boobs done,

get my buns tightened

and maybe, for fun,

I'd get a hair transplant,

to stay looking young.

In keeping with fashion,

put a stud in my tongue.

And when my improvements

were finally made,

I'd have the best body

that's on Medicaid.

Regression

My hands are all gnarled
and mottled with brown.
My laugh lines appear
whenever I frown.
My eyelids are sagging,
my hair's turning white.
I've sprouted chin whiskers
and shrunk some in height.
My body is aging
with each passing day.
But my mind is regressing.
I stay young that way.

Silk Scarves

My legs are slim and girlish.

My breasts are both intact.

I made up in experience

for what my body lacked.

My eyes still twinkle boldly.

I remember how to flirt.

I wear a daring, low cut blouse

and slim, hip hugging skirt.

The one thing age has done to me

I really do despise,

is make my neck all wrinkled,

which I've chosen to disguise,

by using scarves of finest silk

to hide the flesh that's shrunken.

I could be this generation's

Isadora Duncan.

Bionic Woman

My glasses go on my nightstand.
My teeth get soaked in a glass.
My pills get laid out in a saucer,
for indigestion and gas.
I carefully pull off my hairpiece
which goes on its Styrofoam head.
I'm the bionic woman,
getting ready for bed.

Footloose and Fancy Free

Remember when we shopped for shoes

and focused on the style:

wedgies, platforms, backless heels,

all bought to make men smile.

Sexy straps and pointy toes

and shiny patent leather,

we'd show them off in rain or snow,

regardless of the weather.

Now all I care about is fit,

and if the heels are low,

and if they fit my bunions

and my painful hammertoe.

So what if they aren't sexy?

At my age, what's the use?

I'd rather walk in comfort

than give my feet abuse.

So if my Easy Spirit® shoes

don't make your eyes go "wow,"

it's not your ugly, calloused feet

that wear them, anyhow.

Horsing Around

My doctor says, "cut down on fat."

I guess that I could live with that.

He also says to exercise,

but I've already skinny thighs.

Sweets are a no-no on his list

(the thing I really can't resist)

He thinks that I eat too much salt.

Talk to Lays®. It's not my fault.

I know I'm healthy as a horse.

(But they live 20 years, of course.)

Stretch Marks

When I was young and foolish,

we gals were burning bras,

tossing out our girdles

and going for Lamaze.

Yes, we were young and supple -

no stretch marks, cellulite,

unsightly fat deposits,

wrinkles or crows feet.

Today I opt for good support.

No fancy bras for me.

'tis Lycra® that has given back

the shape I used to be.

THE FACTS
OF WIFE

Golf Widow

We retired to the mountains
to live a peaceful life.
Now I'm a golf widow
instead of a wife.

My husband isn't strong enough
to help in any way,
but he can drag his clubs around
18 holes a day.

He comes home just exhausted
from walking in the sun,
and has the nerve to tell me
that golf is so much fun.

But that's all right, my darling.
Go ahead and chase your balls.
But while you're on the golf course,
I'm hitting all the malls.

Reservations

I do not own a housedress,

nor an apron for my waist.

I buy my pies from the grocer

when I want a taste

of apples or blackberries.

No rolling pin for me.

But I'm as good a baker

as my grandma used to be.

I could make a cake from scratch,

mix cookies in a minute,

complete with chocolate and nuts

or spice and raisins in it.

But why mess up my kitchen

to open up a box?

I'll just relax with some chablis,

kick off my Birkenstocks®

and read until my husband,

who knows my limitations,

reaches for the phone to make

dinner reservations.

Label Fables

My latest hobby is labels.

I read them at the supermart.

I look for all the bad stuff

that goes into my grocery cart.

Trans fat is bad but tastes good,

and so does MSG.

My grocer doesn't carry

a low fat brand of brie.

Sugar's put in everything

that I would want to buy.

Everything that's on the shelf

has chemicals or dye,

or additives, preservatives,

or isn't on my diet.

If they don't make my kind of food,

there's no way I can buy it.

So let me eat my Twinkies®,

my chips and candy bars,

and I won't nag about your beer

and smelly old cigars.

Facts of Wife

When the forecast is gloomy and calling for snow,

it's to the grocery store you must go.

A household must always have things on hand

to whip up a meal, either frozen or canned,

a pantry well stocked with nibbles and snacks,

like chips in their own individual packs.

Stock up on water, an emergency stash

of Oreo cookies® (your own private cache).

Most vital of all, before it is gone,

buy some more paper for everyone's john.

Make sure there is beer on your grocery list,

just to make sure that he won't get pissed.

Yes, happy homemaker, you save the day

by stocking the home when there's snow on the way.

I wonder when parents reveal facts of life,

why don't they spell out the true "facts of wife?"

Queen of the house?

My husband, the executive,
ran a company.
Now that he's retired,
he's trying to run me.

He reorganized the kitchen.
I cannot find a thing.
He claims I'm not efficient,
and he's timed my vacuuming.

He's thrown out things I've needed
just to find some busy work.
With all his rearranging,
he's driving me berserk.

My house was once in order.
I was queen of my domain.
But since my love retired,
he's become a royal pain.

Micro-Management

My husband is a genius.

He can set our VCR.

He sets the clocks around the home

and even in the car.

But he has selective learning

with appliances in the house.

Washer/dryer settings are

left up to the spouse.

The dishwasher's another

puzzle to ignore.

He cannot figure out at all

what the dials are for.

So how come he's so brilliant

at microwaving dinner?

When it comes to eating,

my husband's no beginner.

Volunteering

They sold us on retirement as a worthwhile aim,

and put us out to pasture without a moment's shame.

They wanted someone younger to handle all our work,

and we were free to golf instead of slaving like a jerk.

Now we have a lot of time without a real career,

why is it people always try to make us volunteer?

They want our skills and talent, and ethics, I daresay.

We're working hard as ever but not getting any pay.

We'll gladly serve upon your boards and volunteer our skill,

and for our time and energy, we'll just send you the bill.

"You want it all for free?" you say. "I've nothing else to do?"

I'm very busy concentrating on my mountain view.

Equality

When it comes to sharing housework,
my husband is no slouch.
He willingly helps out a lot
while stretched out on the couch.

His idea of equality
in helping with the chores
is pointing out the things I miss
while I sweep up the floors.

THE
CHANGE
OF LIFE

Yearly Exam

Feet in the stirrups, toes in the air,

I'm flat on my back, and going nowhere.

Knees at right angles, boobs hanging down,

I'm sporting the latest in pink paper gown.

I'm wondering if I used enough Nair®

while the doctor is looking for what isn't there.

Now I don't expect him to find anything,

but just that he's looking is embarrassing.

The older I get, the more doctors I see

each looking at various aspects of me.

I'd rather avoid them like flu or colonics,

relax with a book and drink cold gin and tonics.

Hormonia

Premenstrual Syndrome (PMS)

and all the periodic stress

that gave us cramping and distress

was over long ago.

We're done with flushing,

chocolate stuffing,

bad hair fluffing

moods that come and go.

We're over sweating,

finished fretting,

and coquetting,

stopped our monthly flow.

But when the estrogen gives out

we give a hallelujah shout

and we are finally about

to take life nice and slow...

that's when testosterone kicks in,

growing whiskers on the chin.

It seems that women just can't win.

Our hormones steal the show.

Oh, Lucky Me

In the game of life, I've found a new wrinkle.

Whenever I sneeze, I tend to tinkle.

And though I try, I can't pretend.

The time has come for a Depend®.

I sidle down the grocery aisle,

blushing with embarrassed heat,

praying anyone I know, I will not chance to meet.

Just as I get to the checkout line,

who should be there but a friend of mine.

And as we chat, she's busy eyeing

everything in the cart I'm buying.

Why does it always seem to be

that bad luck has to follow me?

Command Performance

A lady somewhere around 50

thought it would be very nifty

to fall into sleep

without counting sheep

or stooping to anything shifty.

She just needed eight hours rest,

though nine would ideally be best.

But she'd get up to pee

at a quarter to 3,

then toss for an hour, she guessed.

She rested with everything bared,

for she was too warm, she declared.

First she was hot,

and then she was not.

Her thermostat must be impaired.

She tossed and she turned and she fanned.

What she wanted was sleep on demand.

But what is conducive

to sleep is elusive

when menopause is in command.

It's a Guy Thing

Ever notice the things that start with "men?"

Those things that drive us crazy when

we just can't cope.

The end of the rope.

Yes, "mental" starts with "men."

Even "menstrual" starts with men,

and men don't get the cramps, my frien'

or PMS,

but I digress.

We're just discussing men.

And what about "menopause?"

I see a couple of flaws.

While we're getting gray,

they're looking to stray,

and excusing it "just because."

And why is it called "His"terectomy?

It's all just a pain in the neck to me.

But they're good for one thing,

and that's called marrying,

and handing over the check to me.

Changing Times

Feeling witchy? A little twitchy?
And at times you're downright bitchy?
Not to worry. Not to fret.
You aren't over the hill just yet.

So what's a modern gal to do
when the "change" is upon her?
Men-o-pause, it's men-o-pause,
when first blush of youth is a goner.

Getting sweaty? Acting petty?
Craving chocolate and spaghetti?
Boobies sag and waistlines thicken,
and your hairdo takes a lickin'.

So what if we're dumpy and just a bit frumpy
and mornings we tend to be just a bit grumpy.
But never accuse of us fuzzy thinking.
We may be down, but we're not sinking.
(Yet.)

It's His Fault

"Why do my boobs hang down so low?"
I asked my g-y-n.
The doctor looked at me and said,
"it has to do with men."

Men-o, men-o, p-a-u-s-e.
It's not so strange.
It's just the change
that happens eventually.

If you are lucky enough to age,
you can do it with grace.
And yet, without a lift or tuck,
it will surely show on your face.

Your waist gets thick, your legs get thin,
it's hard to sleep, and then
when your hair starts turning gray,
you blame it all on men.

Padding

When I first got my periods
I wore a belt around my middle
that firmly held a pad in place
(which chafed my legs a little).

We've come a long, long way since then,
with tampons, pads and birth control.
There's freedom from that time of month
along our southern hole.

Now that we're done with PMS
and cramps and monthly bloat,
the curse is finally over
but there is no time to gloat.

We may not have to suffer
with a belt around the middle,
but now we have to wear a pad
because we tend to piddle.

Technologically
Challenged

Reaching Out

When I was little, Spam® was food. Blackberries went in pie.

An apple was a piece of fruit. And we all cooked with Spry®.

Well, times have changed a bit, I guess.

Phone booths are hard to find.

We carry cell phones everywhere, but I don't really mind.

Reaching out to touch someone in this electronic age

is getting so much harder when these gadgets are the rage.

Won't someone please just hug me? An email's not the same.

I want to be much more to you than some old dot com name.

Send me valentines and notes, not email cutesy poo,

I'm too old to get involved with learning something new.

Forget about computers and electronic text.

I need some personal contact. Do you think I'm oversexed?

Bells and Whistles

My appliances all yell at me and order me around.

When my dryer clicks to "off," I hear a buzzing sound.

Even my refrigerator scolds me when the door

stays open for too long a time. So how can I explore

what's on the lower shelving, without its noxious beeping?

I need the time to rearrange the leftovers I'm keeping.

My oven beeps when heating. My microwave goes "ding."

It seems that everything I own lets out a noisy "ping."

I hate the bells and whistles that fill my little kitchen.

I liked it better way back when appliances weren't bitchin'.

Surfin' Turf

I was a tomboy through and through, in my younger years.

I suffered sprains and bruises, and cried my share of tears.

I did a lot of damage in my hyperactive youth.

I dislocated my big toe and broke off my front tooth.

But now I'm sedentary – I'll go to any length

to move with quiet dignity and conserve my strength.

So who knew I could suffer an injury so dumb

just using my computer? They call it "surfer's thumb."

Add that to my bursitis, my hip and knee distress.

Just sitting still, I'm diagnosed a post-traumatic mess.

So I won't send you emails, and don't you send them back.

I'm busy nurturing my joints and sacroiliac.

Gizmo a go go

When did I get to be so smart that I can see the flaws

in everybody else I know? It truly gives me pause.

I could tell the doctor why my sore toe isn't gout,

and I could tell the Pentagon how to go about

solving all our problems, and how to win the war.

I have lived through history and what went on before.

I'm right about the weather. I know when it will rain.

I don't trust the weatherman, but I can trust my pain.

If I'm so smart, I find it just a little bit ironic

that I am totally perplexed by all things electronic.

I can run appliances without thinking twice.

I know how to fix the world, and I can give advice.

But I can't program the remote on my new TV set.

I have to ask my grandson how to surf the internet.

In spite of everything I know, I wouldn't have much strife

if there weren't all these gizmos in my prehistoric life.

Iron Age

I used to iron everything
from a hanky to a sheet.
But with the newer fabrics now
my iron's obsolete.
My ironing board is stored away.
It, too, is out of favor,
along with clothes pins, starch and soap.
My dryer's a lifesaver.
No more wringer/washer tubs
or dryer lines for me.
While my machines are working,
I have the morning free.
I head out to the golf course
with the only iron I need,
and chip my ball onto the green
with awe-inspiring speed.
An iron's useful after all
for eliminating stress,
so long as it is not employed
to crease or steam or press.

MEMORY LANE

Morning Routine

Did I swallow my pills?

I just can't recall.

I was thinking about them…

I came down the hall,

went into the bathroom,

washed hands and face,

looked in the mirror,

combed hair in place,

went into the bedroom

to make up the bed,

made sure that the dog

and the cat both were fed,

washed up the dishes,

watered the plants,

folded clean laundry,

and ironed my pants,

sat down at the desk

to pay all my bills.

But did I remember

to swallow my pills?

Perks and Quirks

Now that I'm a senior, I get a lot of perks.

People smile knowingly, forgiving all my quirks.

I can get away with insulting checkout clerks.

If other people did that, they'd just be labeled jerks.

I can miss appointments, and get excused with smirks,

when I shake my wrist and say,

"my watch no longer works."

I won't let on that I can't see the numbers on its face,

or say I'm late because my keys weren't in their usual place.

So if I seem forgetful, or addled just a bit,

perhaps I can't remember what I don't want to admit.

I Remember You

I remember your face
and the last time we met.
It's only your name
that I tend to forget.
I know who you dated
when we were in school,
and that red bikini
you wore at the pool.
I danced at your wedding
some decades ago.
There are so many things
that I used to know.
I can remember
your past oh, so well.
It's just that my present
has gone all to hell.

Girl Talk

Don't tell me about your facelift,

or hernia repair,

or any of your surgeries.

I honestly don't care.

Don't brag about your children –

the ones I've never met.

Don't show me all their pictures.

Their names, I'll just forget.

And please don't tell me gossip

or your husband's bedroom style.

Any men I've ever known

have beat him by a mile.

I can't remember why we're friends

or how we got together,

but if you want to stay my friend,

just focus on the weather.

Errands

I was running low on a couple of things

so I left for the grocery store.

And while I was out, I stopped at the bank,

got gas and a lock for the door.

I also bought stamps and picked up some pills,

a mop for cleaning my floor.

I came home exhausted, only to find

I forgot to go to the store.

uncertainty

I'm driving to visit a girl friend,
my eyes on the road straight ahead.
A thought pops into my wand'ring mind
and I'm suddenly filled with dread.

Did I really turn off the oven?
Is my coffeepot still plugged in?
Did I recall shutting off my washer
after it started to spin?

I don't remember rechecking
to see if I locked the front door.
My memory stops when I'm driving.
It's happened so often before.

I return to the house and start checking.
Everything's off and secure.
I knew it before I departed.
So why am I never quite sure?

Safe Places

I cannot find my pocket book,

my glasses or my key.

I know I put them somewhere safe,

but for the life of me,

I simply can't remember

the place that "safe" would be.

I've looked in all the bedrooms,

and underneath the chair,

and all the kitchen countertops,

but they aren't anywhere.

They're never in the places

that I think they ought to be.

The thing I lose most often

seems to be my memory.

MUSINGS

Machismo

Men used to whistle when I passed, admiring all of me.

But now they look the other way, and don't like what they see.

My legs, once firm and curvy, are filled with ropy veins,

resembling more a road map than advertisement for Hanes®.

So they may not be beautiful, but I'll bet they have more hair

than the baldies do who whistle, who used to stop and stare.

I'll bet my legs are slimmer than the road construction crew

who took the time to leer at me when I was twenty-two.

They may be lined and dimpled like a deep dish apple pie,

but I don't seek approval from just any macho guy.

So fella, when I walk your way, show a little class,

and I will promise not to giggle at your sorry ass.

Senioritis

The weather's cold and damp today. I've got the miseries.

My lumbago's aching, there's arthritis in my knees,

my shoulder hurts, I think I've got the symptoms of bursitis.

My husband looked at me and said,

"You've got the 'senioritis.'"

I know I'm getting older, with minor aches and pains,

but since my grandma's golden years,

we gals have made some gains.

Hot flashes have been redesigned.

Now they're "power surges."

And we don't have insomnia, but "melatonin urges."

We all stopped counting calories and went low carb instead.

We're too busy to stay home and bake some gingerbread.

We're running to the doctor, the psychotherapist,

the club for lunch, the hair salon and the podiatrist.

We volunteer our time and skill (especially our hearts).

Refer to us as ladies, please, instead of "those old farts."

Mammograms

What they do to women, well
it ought to be a crime.
I got a post card in the mail:
"it's booby crunching time."

They place a boob upon a slab
of steel as cold as ice,
and tell us not to breathe while we
are squeezed within this vice.

It's diagnostic warfare
in the battle of the sexes.
But it's the rank unfairness
that particularly vexes.

If men were told they had to have
their family jewels compressed,
their scientists would fast invent
a kinder, gentler test.

Peekaboo

Once I was tall and willowy, 5' 6" in stocking feet.

But every day I find that I'm becoming more petite.

My ears are getting longer, but my fingernails won't grow.

My hair is turning grayer, and I've lost that youthful glow.

My feet don't touch the pedal of my latest automobile.

I'm not ready to quit driving, but I can't see o'er the wheel.

Why can't they build an SUV for someone who's my size?

To see and reach the pedal, I have to improvise.

There's a cushion that I sit on, and one to prop me up,

and one to blow up in my face in case of a smash-up.

So if you cannot see me, it's a cinch I can't see you.

Just wave me past the stop sign, as I go sailing through.

Precious Darlings

I always smile at children,

and babies who are cute

(even when they're screaming

and their tantrums are a beaut.)

I like them even better

when they nag and cry and whine.

It's then that I am happiest

that these kids are not mine.

I revel in their acting out

as kids are wont to do,

and I thank all the gods above

that they belong to you.

Snail Mail

I used to get letters in the mail from friends and family,

and I looked forward to the ones hand addressed to me.

The art of writing letters has somehow all been lost.

I miss the stationery made of linen, and embossed.

Now there's instant messaging and email to my friends.

I save the cost of postage and keep up with all the trends.

But since I have retired, the mail that I receive

wants me to plan my funeral so loved ones will not grieve,

or buy some term insurance, or choices for health care,

nursing home insurance, or supplements to spare.

So even though they send me mail, I have no need for buying.

I'm focusing on my living, while they're focusing on my dying.

Moi?

Little old ladies walking along,

bundled against the breeze.

They're wearing a sweater,

a scarf and a hat,

and the weather is 90 degrees.

They carry umbrellas in case it might rain,

wear boots that will help them stay dry.

There isn't a cloud to be seen up above

in a beautiful, blue summer sky.

What's left in their closets when they venture out?

They're wearing whatever they've got.

I feel like sweating just looking their way.

Wouldn't you think they are hot?

I reach for my jacket and head for the door,

and look in the mirror and see

the reflection of someone who's all bundled up.

Could that little old lady be me?

Fun in the Sun

I watch the kids outside at play

with a ball and bat,

running barefoot in the grass.

I used to be like that.

I couldn't wait to get a tan.

I'd sit out in the sun,

with just a dab of suntan cream

till I was overdone.

Now I see things differently.

I know the sun can hurt.

I load up on the sunscreen,

and wear a long sleeved shirt.

And when I go out walking,

I wear a lot of clothes,

put on my darkest glasses,

and cover up my nose.

With all the stuff that I put on,

to guard me from the rays,

how's a gal supposed to flirt

with anyone these days?

Hair

I'm shopping at Wal-Mart wondering what
I should do to cover my gray.
I used to be a warm chestnut brown,
but I'm salt and pepper today.
Should I go red, or maybe ash blonde?
It's hard to make a decision.
I'd love to look like the models I see in the ads on television.
Their locks are luxurious, curly and thick.
Mine are regrettably thin.
So I look at the colors and brands on the shelf,
and I'm wondering where to begin.
If I had the patience, and I could be brave,
I think I'd go au naturel.
I'd wear my gray proudly and hold up my head,
and pretend I'm a true femme fatale.
In the end I wimp out, and reach for a box.
This is the moment of truth.
Then a girl with pink hair comes by and I stare.
What's happening to all our youth?
I guess I don't want to be young after all.
I'll settle for brown and look smart.
My hair doesn't have to be candy cane pink
just to prove that I'm still young at heart.

Reflection

I look in the mirror and I see
my mother looking back at me.
When she was 60, she was old
and had a tremor uncontrolled.
She wore a housedress every day
and sported locks of silver gray.
I run around in sexy jeans
and act just like I'm in my teens.
Miss Clairol® is my dearest friend.
I follow every style trend.
I watch my diet and my weight
and everyone says I look great.
I feel so young, but what I see
is her face looking back at me.

Garden Fantasies

I wouldn't mind a garden, but the roses all have thorns,

and weeding out the flowerbeds tends to hurt my corns,

and spreading mulch would aggravate my lower vertebrae,

and fertilizer costs more money than I want to pay.

And then I'd have to water all the tender little shoots,

and worry if the weather would destroy their little roots.

I'd worry about aphids, and mealy worms and slugs,

and if my garden had enough bees and lady bugs.

I ought to have a garden, but the work's too hard for me.

I'll buy my flowers by the pot at the grocery.

If anybody asks me where I got that luscious bloom,

I'll smile and whisper softly,

"from my late husband's tomb."

Preparedness

My morning constitutional
should be a mile or more,
but I have all that I can do
to make it out the door.
I dab some sunscreen on my face,
grab a hat for shade,
my walking stick, sunglasses and
a bottle of Gatorade®,
an energy bar, a cardigan,
a tube of liniment cream,
some safety pins in case I fall
and rip a vital seam,
a pocket full of bandages,
an extra pair of socks,
my keys, ID and pocket change,
a jacket and Reebocks®,
my cell phone and my MP3,
some pain pills for my gout.
Even before I start to walk,
I feel all tuckered out.

Queen of the Road

Little old ladies

a scant five feet tall,

driving their Cadillacs®

down to the mall.

What do they want

with that much in horsepower,

when they go no faster

than five miles an hour?

When I'm an old lady,

my hair won't be blue.

I'll be drag racing

when I'm 82.

No Lincoln® or Lexus®

or Caddy® for me.

I'll be queen of the road

in my big SUV.

Baggage

When I was young, my purse was filled
with things I thought I'd need:
make-up, hairbrush, spray cologne,
a racy book to read.
These days, my purse's contents look
more like a pharmacy.
I don't leave home without some pills
to keep me company.
I've pills for my arthritic pain,
eye drops for dry eyes,
tablets made for gas relief
and to neutralize
stomach acid when I eat,
a hemorrhoidal wipe,
and of course, a plastic bag
for all the rolls I swipe.

My Pharmacy

Whoever said when getting old
we'd reach our golden age,
was either young or witless,
but certainly no sage.
I take a pill for this and that
to keep my pressure low,
to keep my thyroid stable and
maintain my youthful glow.
I take a hormone supplement
and vitamins galore.
My cupboard looks increasingly
like a health food store.
With all the pills I have to take
to keep me feeling great,
there isn't any room for food
so why am I gaining weight?